THE
SEVERN
VALE
IN OLD PHOTOGRAPHS

THE
SEVERN
VALE
IN OLD PHOTOGRAPHS

COLLECTED BY
ALAN SUTTON

ALAN SUTTON
1986

Alan Sutton Publishing Limited
Brunswick Road · Gloucester

First published 1986

British Library Cataloguing in Publication Data

Sutton, Alan
The Severn vale in old photographs.
1. Gloucestershire—Description and
travel—Views 2. Severn, River, Valley
(Wales and England)—Description and
travel—Views
I. Title
914.24′1   DA670.G5
ISBN 0-86299-271-0

Front cover illustration:
From left to right: John Merrett, Mr. Hollingworth and Charles Cooper, schoolmaster at
Arlingham. Boys, left to right: Thomas Martin, James Edwards, John Carter and Ivor
Goulding. Seated: Frank Pockett and Harold Withers.

Typesetting and origination by
Alan Sutton Publishing Limited.
Printed in Great Britain.

CONTENTS

The Stockham Family; the couple at the back are Anne and Nathanial Stockham, the two girls are Lizzie and Carrie Stockham. The couple in the middle are unknown. (See page 61).

INTRODUCTION

In the conceptual stages of this book I was considering the title of *The Horseshoe and the Severn Vale in Old Photographs*, but this was too cumbersome and so the 'Horseshoe' was dropped. And yet in a way this was a pity, because the horseshoe in the river makes a marvellous natural feature which cries out to be emphasised.

The boundaries within which I have collected photographs for this book are the River Severn in the west, the Bristol Road in the east, Hempsted in the north and Frampton in the south. This basically comprises the north-western section of the Vale of Berkeley. Although this area is by no means unique it has features found nowhere else in Gloucestershire other than in a similar sized tract between Gloucester and Tewkesbury. For instance, walk or drive only three miles east and you are in the hybrid area of brick and Cotswold stone. Three miles to the south and you reach the hybrid area of brick and sandstone; to the west over the river there is a mixture of brick and indigenous stone, but in the Severn Vale there is only soft local brick, or timber, wattle and daub. The vernacular style is easily apparent. A warm style in mellow brick with clay pantiles, or sometimes slate in houses built after 1820. The common Frampton material is the flat clay tile, often replacing thatch which has by and large disappeared over the last hundred years. Wattle and daub has generally disappeared in England, unlike Normandy where timber buildings still exist in large numbers in this style. In the Severn Vale, as in other parts of England, the wattle and daub has been generally replaced by brick infills, painted white.

The Severn Vale, although not isolated, retains an insular identity created through geography and circumstances. In the west the river is a natural boundary, and in the east the world rushes by, north and south, via the A38 and the M5. In medieval times Frampton and Arlingham were well into the mainstream, as one of the major routes of the county was the road to the Arlingham Passage and on to the Forest of Dean and Wales. In the eighteenth and early nineteenth centuries there were further bursts of activitity during the building of the Stroudwater, and then the Gloucester and Sharpness canals. But as canal activity dropped and railways were routed elsewhere (several schemes for crossing the river locally never came to anything due to Admiralty opposition) the Vale became a backwater, retaining the charm lost by so many other country areas.

Arlingham in particular makes a fascinating study. Surrounded by water on three sides, the village has developed an identity and dialect of its own. From Framilode up to Elmore the character of the area remains the same, as if the building of the canal in 1827 strengthened the sense of independence amongst the local population. In the late eighteenth century two studies were made of the county. William Marshall in his *Rural Economy of Glocestershire* says of the area that

> Farm labourers are sufficiently numerous – they are noticeable as being simple, inoffensive, unintelligent, and apparently slow. How different from the farm labourers of Norfolk!
>
> Their wages are very low in money; being only one shilling a day. But, in drink, shamefully exorbitant. Six quarts a day, the common allowance; frequently two gallons: sometimes nine or ten quarts; or an unlimited quantity.

If Marshall is to be believed, the agricultural work of the Vale was conducted in an on-going alcoholic stupor. He wrote his account in 1789; but ten years before, Samuel Rudder had made a trip around the Vale in preparation for his county history and noted the following:

> [Arlingham] The air is made very unwholesome by the copious humid exhalations from the river, and from the lands which are so frequently overflowed. This occasions inveterate headaches, and all those possible disorders incident to a low, damp situation, in which the poorer sort of people, who live hard, have so manifestly the disadvantage in point of health . . .
>
> Notwithstanding the situation of this village upon the Severn, fish is not so commonly the food of its inhabitants as might be imagined, on account of the great price it usually bears. Salmon, in the greatest plenty of the season, commonly sells for threepence halfpenny or fourpence a pound. I took some notice, about two years ago, of an eel, just taken, five feet ten inches long, and twenty-eight pounds weight, which a butcher was stripping at this village, and thought it a great curiosity; but several persons informed me, that there was

nothing extraordinary in it, as a man, then living in the place, had taken one which weighed six score pounds. The flesh of this animal was sold to the poor people at twopence a pound. It was very white, but of a strong, nasty smell, and must be unwholesome food.

[Saul] The air is rendered impure and unwholesome by the copious vapours and exhalations rising from the Severn, and from the low lands which are constantly drowned by floods and spring tides, which particularly affect Saul, Moreton and Fretherne. Yet here I was told, that this village was perfectly healthy, though it appeared to be far otherwise, from the palid countenances of those I conversed with, who allowed, however, that the two other above-mentioned neighbouring villages were greatly afflicted with agues and asthmatic disorders. On the contrary, the good people of Moreton assured me, that they were themselves free from those disorders, but that Saul and Fretherne were very subject to them. Thus wisely has providence reconciled mankind to their various situations ...

What with the alcohol and the 'exhalations from the river' it is surprising that anyone survived in this area at all, yet alone thrived. Generally, from the late sixteenth through to the nineteenth centuries, the Vale ceased to be arable and became prime dairy land, the home of the Double Gloucester, renowned throughout the world. The ridge and furrow of medieval times remains to this day, although not now so pronounced. Marshall noted in 1789 that, when standing in one furrow, it was sometimes impossible to see a plough team working over the ridge in the next furrow.

Against this agricultural background, our photographic trip begins. The earliest pictures are from the 1870s, only eighty years after Marshall made his comments on the effects of alcohol. The peak of photographic activity was between 1890 and 1910, when photographers/entrepreneurs published their postcard views of villages. Without these photographic records, our knowledge of the area as it was at that time would be greatly diminished.

In recent years change has accelerated. The A38 has become a fast, wide road, and not the dirt track it is shown as being on page 79. Houses have sprung up, the aerial photographs of Arlingham, Frampton, Hardwicke and Quedgeley show how the housing density has increased since 1960.

With 'progress', motor transport, and this accelerated style of living, the village atmosphere has by and large disappeared. Until World War II, public transport was by bus or, in the case of Frampton and Saul, by boats such as *Lapwing* (see page 98). Village atmosphere was very different. There were hardly any 'strangers', and most locals had nicknames, names in common usage above and beyond Christian names. On page 120 we have 'Podding' Leach, a name he was given after writing an essay at school in which he put 'podding' instead of 'pudding'. A simple schoolboy slip that ended up being his name for life.

Characters abounded, Bill Coole the landlord of the Horseshoes is shown in the picture below. He was famous for his practical jokes, and on one occasion he announced that he had in his possession a 'water otter', and challenged any dog to catch it. Along came poachers, farmers, and other disreputable characters so that the green was soon alive with dogs and spectators. Out came Coole with a sack over his shoulder, he slowly waded into the pond and emptied the contents of the sack and then beat a hasty retreat. Instantly the dogs were loosed, but it soon became apparent that there was no wild animal, dead or alive in that pond. Eventually the 'water 'otter' was fished out, and found to be an old kettle. Luckily for Coole the crowd saw the joke.

The pictures in this book should prove to be of interest to young and old in the Severn Vale, and as every year passes by and change accelerates further, the illustrations should prove to be of greater interest to the generations that follow. Sadly many people destroyed old photographs thinking them to be meaningless rubbish. I hope that in the publishing of this book I have managed to save photographic images that may otherwise have been designated to the bonfires of the future.

ALAN SUTTON
November 1986

Outside the Whitminster Hotel; left to right; —?—, Percy Prout, —?—, Bill Coole and Arthur Lewis.

Arlingham
and
Fretherne

ARLINGHAM PASSAGE c.1900. This is cheating a little; the picture here is of the Newnham side, not Arlingham. Tom Phillips is fending the boat off, ready to get back to the Arlingham side to start our photographic trip.

THE PASSAGE from the Arlingham side, tracks from the ferry in the sand and mud at low tide.

THE NEW INN, 1953, now known as *The Old Passage*. This picture is from a colour transparency taken by Bernard Shaw, long before the demise of the elm trees.

ARLINGHAM DRUM AND FIFE BAND c.1900. From left to right, seated; Ralph, Edward and Paul Greenway (not necessarily in that order). Second row; Gilbert Wright, Samuel Aldridge, Samuel Greenway (later the Frampton Blacksmith), —?— Greenway, C.O. Cooper, bandmaster. Third row; Richard Dangerfield, Alfred Holder, Albert Dangerfield, Bill Creed. Back row; —?— Greenway, Jesse Greenway, Thomas Willavise and Albert Merrett.

A VIEW OF ARLINGHAM CROSS, the Red Lion on the right, the sign for the Bell Inn on the left. Photograph c.1905.

MRS. WHITE ON HER 100TH BIRTHDAY c.1915

BOER WAR VICTORY CELEBRATIONS outside the Red Lion, 1901.

HIGH STREET, ARLINGHAM c.1950. From left to right; Judith Wells, Nellie Holder, Pam Wright and Nellie Greenway.

Right: ARLINGHAM FROM THE AIR, 1967. Note the medieval ridge and furrow all around the village. The ruins of the dovecote are in the field opposite the church.

ARLINGHAM DRUM AND FIFE BAND c.1915. From left to right; Heber Greenway, Leslie Woodman, William Merrett, Charles Greenway, Charlie Butt, Frank Fletcher, Percy Aldridge, Sidney Merrett, Thomas Martin, Joseph Greenway, C.O. Cooper, Stanley Merrett, Ira (Jack) Aldridge, Ivor Goulding, George Greenway, Moreton Merrett, Harold Smith, Roland Woodman, Gilbert Wright, Harold Withers, Thomas Burcher and George Sendell.

SOME OF THE ARLINGHAM VOLUNTEERS, c.1905. Left to right; Maurice Merrett, C.O. Cooper, John Hayward, Robert Hayward, Gilbert Wright, Edwin Withers and on horseback W.P. Merrett.

SLOWWE HOUSE; Squire Sayers' daughters' wedding, c.1878.

THE REVD. AND MRS. BEAVIS' GOLDEN WEDDING, inviting the Mothers Union to tea c.1926. From left to right; Sarah Pockett, Sarah Greenway, Kate Price, Gladys Vernon, Flossie Price, Lillie Hayward, —?— Dangerfield, Gladys Harding, Mary Holder, Mary Weekes, —?— Page, —?— Stone, Revd. Henry Beavis, Joyce Merrett, Lilian Merrett, —?— Harrison, Lisa Young, Rosa Beavis, Olive Wright, Nora Aldridge, Bessie Aldridge, —?— Asher, Anita Holder, Nora Shaw, Carrie Butt, Eleanor Withers, Michael Curtis, and Charlotte Curtis.

ARLINGHAM COURT c.1860. This is the oldest photograph in the book and shows the Court before the serious deterioration caused the roof to collapse.

ARLINGHAM COURT c.1880 with the roof on the east wing fallen in.

ARLINGHAM COURT c.1880, the south-west side. Within two years of this picture the building had been demolished.

RECTORY FARM c.1905, the home of the Wilcox family.

ARLINGHAM CHURCH, 1904; Hella Beavis centre, James Butt on horseback. The church tower was built between 1373–1375. One Nicholas Wyshongre, mason, contracted on 25 November 1372 to complete the tower in three years. 12 feet were to be built in each year and he was to be paid 17 shillings and one bushel of wheat for each foot completed.

THE DOVECOTE, January 1942. This picture was taken on a 15 shilling 2A Box Brownie by Bernard Shaw. Although the sun is low and not ideally placed, the picture is interesting as the elms, dovecote and now the cedar have all gone.

W.P. AND EMMA MERRETT, C.1900.

BERNARD AND NORA SHAW outside Clapsgate, now the village post office, 1917.

W.P. MERRETT outside Wilston House, High Street c.1900.

SHOEMAKERS SHOP at the bottom of High Street, St. Augustine's Cottage (now demolished). In the doorway, George Wright, centre, — ? — French, right, Edwin Hayward. Photograph c.1880.

RICK BUILDING ON PUCKPOOL FARM c.1890.

THE BUTT FAMILY AND RETAINERS c.1906. From left to right standing; Calvert Taylor, — ? — Woodman(?), Leonard Gardiner, — ? — Markey, George Butt (killed during World War I), Isaac Woodman (senior), Bessy Woodman, Frank Ryder, Isaac Woodman (junior) and William Gardiner. Front row; Carrie Butt, Charlie Butt, James Butt and Ada Butt.

RICK BUILDING AT COURT FARM c.1914. The couple at the back right hand side are William and Lilian Spring.

MISS ADA BUTT (right hand side) with bicycle c.1915.

LIONEL E. DARELL AND SIR LIONEL DARELL with the Fretherne Foot Beagles outside the south door of Fretherne Court, c.1910.

Baden Powell would have been proud of them! A group of local scouts outside the Court c.1910. Notice the domestics in the doorway trying to get in on the picture.

MAY DAY CELEBRATIONS in the west garden of Fretherne Court c.1906. Notice the sailor suits on the little boys to the right.

A GARDEN PARTY AT FRETHERNE COURT c.1917, possibly to celebrate Lionel E. Darell's safe return from fighting the Turks in the Sinai Desert. Revd. Beavis seated to the left of the picture.

THE EAST WING OF FRETHERNE COURT with the conservatory and ornamental ponds, c.1895. Fretherne Court started as a humble rectory, but Revd. Sir Lionel William Darell built on many extra reception rooms, a ballroom, billiard room, water towers and halls to make the rectory into a substantial country house.

FRETHERNE SCHOOL c.1910. Front row; Judy Jardine, Grace Greenway, Winifred Greenway, Vera Greenway, Miss Lucy Greenway (teacher), Daisy Clutterbuck, Sidney Gough, Nellie Gough and Charlie Berry. Middle row; Kate Clutterbuck, Zoe Clutterbuck, Cassie Coates, Edie Gough, Mary Berry and Maud Berry. Back row; Ida Jardine, Willie Jardine, Willie Clutterbuck, Edie Jones, Ethel Jones, Violet Woolford, Fred Hillman and Rose Hillman.

THE LODGE TO FRETHERNE COURT c.1910.

THE WEST FACE OF FRETHERNE COURT c.1905.

THE SOUTH FACE OF FRETHERNE COURT c.1905.

THE DEMOLITION OF FRETHERNE COURT in 1926. After Sir Lionel's death 17 February 1919, the estate had to be split up amongst the seven surviving children with provisions for his widow.

"It was very sad, but Fretherne Court had no modern requirements, no central heating, and they say we used to burn a ton of coal a day there ... no electricity although my uncle had advocated this so many years before, the kitchens about a quarter-of-a-mile, so to speak, from the dining rooms, water supply very indifferent, only one or two bathrooms, and the drainage system! ..." Sir Lionel E. Darell, 1950.

The Court with 1,100 acres including several smaller mansions and farms was sold in one lot to Mr. Alfred Daniels of Gloucester and subsequently sold off in portions. The Court was sold for building materials.

STAFF AT THE REDDINGS c.1908. At the back, Charlie Etherington and Arthur Hillman. The names of the female domestics are not known. The owner of the Reddings was Major George Venner, killed during World War I.

FRETHERNE ROAD.

THE TURNPIKE at the junction of Fretherne Road c.1890. The board next to the window gave the rates of tolls for different forms of traffic, although tolls had long ceased to be levied.

Saul Lodge.

TWO VIEWS OF SAUL LODGE in 1906. Lionel E. Darell moved here in 1904 after his marriage. It included 14 acres of grounds and was bought for him by his father Sir Lionel Darell as a wedding present. At the time of the Court sale, 200 acres was kept back and added to the Saul Lodge estate.

Frampton-on-Severn

BRIDGE HOUSE, FRAMPTON.

Canal Bridge Frampton on Severn

Two views of the Gloucester & Sharpness Canal at Fretherne Bridge c.1900. The canal was finally completed in 1827 after a troubled financial history. When it opened it could take vessels up to 600 tons and was the largest canal of its type in the country. The elaborate bridge houses date from the 1840s.

With Doric columns (wooden!) and pediment, they reflected the commercial success of the canal at that time. The design has been attributed to Robert Mylne, but it should be noted that they were built over thirty years after his death in 1811.

FRETHERNE BRIDGE c.1900. The ships on the right probably belonged to Alexander Watkins (see page 47). Kimberley house on the far right had just been built by this time.

FRETHERNE BRIDGE c.1915, S.S. Opal being pulled by tug.

HIS MAJESTY'S SUBMARINE H49 at Fretherne Bridge after paying a courtesy visit to Gloucester 20 March 1937. Note the addition of all the Cadbury buildings since the 1915 photograph.

FRAMPTON GALA 1913.

Two more pictures of Frampton Gala, 1913. Henry Clifford in the foreground with a stick. He was shot in the head and killed by a Turkish sniper in the Sinai Desert, January 1917. Major Clifford was in the Gloucestershire Yeomanry along with Lionel Darell.

LEONARD POCKET outside Westmont some time before 1913. Where his trap is standing later became a coal yard. Alexandra Cottage is behind him.

LAKE HOUSE c.1910

ALEXANDER WATKINS outside Westmont some time after 1913. Captain Watkins started his working life as a trowman's boy and rose to command two trows. On retiring from active seafaring he bought an old Bridgwater ketch the *Selina Jane* built in 1872. He owned various vessels including *Kindly Light,* an iron ketch sunk by submarine gunfire in January 1917. Captain Watkins died in 1935, one of the last of the seafaring men of Arlingham, Saul and Frampton. Along with Captain Hugh Shaw of Arlingham who was the last owner of sailing ships on the estuary, he generated much of the spirit of the area – an area mixed with sea-going and inland waterway cargo carrying; alas an era given over to heavy lorries.

Overleaf, pages 48 & 49. FRAMPTON-ON-SEVERN from the north 13 May 1967. Note the general lack of houses, especially down Bridge Road.

THE DENHALLS c.1890. Now transmogrified and incorporated into a larger structure as *Wisma Mulia*.

ON THE SPORTS FIELD c.1920, Cadburys in the background. From left to right; F. Wilkes, —?—, J. Wellings (General Manager), Albert Daw, Arthur Berry, Harry Marsters, S. Leatherland, Bill Gabb, —?—, Ted Abbey, —?—, Les Hunt and Ernie Westwood.

CADBURYS' ATHLETIC CRICKET CLUB, 1925, with tea ladies. Top row, left to right; Mrs. Westwood, Mrs. J. Wellings, Mrs. Walter Hunt, Mrs. D. Stapleton, — ? —, Mrs. H. Mills, — ? —. Standing; Joe Westwood, Fred Franklin, Frank Pullin, Bill Daw, Dan Stapleton, Fred Marsters, Harold Mills, Joe Marsters and Arthur Lawrence. Seated; Herbert Bolton, Jack Wellings, Ralph Hazel, E.P. Tudor (Captain), Harold Hunt, Charlie Webb and Albert Daw. Front; Charles Weaver and Miss Mary Wellings.

CORONATION DAY, JUNE 1911. Frampton Scouts show their prowess at bridge construction on the Green.

FRAMPTON UNITED AFC 1946-47 season, photographed outside the Bell, from left to right, seated; Guy Ayland, Mervyn Davis, Dick Brazington, Walter Walden, Jim Leach, Reg Davis and Les Loomes. Child in centre; Malcolm Davis. Second row; Charles Weaver, Ken Peacey, Percy Sharp, Arthur Stapleton, Stan Dando, Brian Pollard, Milton Tudor, Frank Halling and Reg Barge.
Back row; George Tudor, Alec Webb, Bob Davis, Les Ball, Fred Pitman, Boyd Dando, Fred Hill and Bill Ings.

PERCY BRADLEY c.1908, a Frampton builder for over half a century.

FRAMPTON-ON-SEVERN under 16s football team, 26 August 1966. From left to right standing; Robert Leach, Kevin O'Neill, John Colcombe, Richard Parsons, Steve Barnfield and Robin Loomes. Front row, left to right; Colin O'Connor, Graham Hogg, Alan Jones, John Barnfield and Graham Naylor.

WILLIAM MEADOWS c.1900. After serving an apprenticeship as a baker William Meadows worked for Wards, grocers in Frampton. In 1914 he worked at the munitions factory at Slimbridge and then moved to Cadburys in 1916. He was the first pensioner of Cadburys at the Frampton site.

KATE PHIPPS, later Kate Meadows c. 1900 with her dogs Mick and Mack. For several years Kate was a parlourmaid at Parklands, Whitminster.

THE BELL with horse drawn delivery wagons c.1900. Apart from the pillars and portico the scene is very similar today excepting the car park and fence.

Looking down the Perryway to the Bell c.1900.

FRAMPTON FEAST 21 August 1916 – halfway through the Battle of the Somme. How many Frampton lads were involved in Haig's futile onslaught whilst their younger brothers and sisters were in this picture?

Facing the Bell, 1947.

THE GREEN AND THE TOP SHOP, 1915.

THE TOP SHOP c.1920.

WELLS ALEXANDER WATKINS AND BILL GOODMAN outside the Top Shop c.1905.

FRAMPTON MANOR FARM c.1905.

Communal paddling 1901.

An enlargement of the notice in the top right picture. 'Any person found throwing ashes or any kind of rubbish on the Green, or stones or any thing else into the ponds will be prosecuted.

H.I. Clifford'

FRAMPTON POST OFFICE c.1895. Nathanial Stockham built the new front to the shop c.1870. Before the Poor Law of 1836, Poole House was the Frampton Workhouse. In the doorway, Carrie Stockham, Lizzie Stockham plus one.

A later view of the Green c.1920, looking north.

Above: cottages to the east of the Green, some now demolished, 1906.

Right: HAWK MEWS, Frampton Manor Farm, 1901.

Far right: If this was a painting it would have been by Helen Allingham, with a small girl in bonnet and a wicker basket! Instead it is a photograph taken in 1900 of some of Frampton's prettiest cottages. The cottages look beautiful, but conditions inside would not be to the modern taste!

THE FRAMPTON RIVIERA 1906.

MR. J. WATHEN, Chairman of the parish council, receiving the Bledisloe Cup for the best kept village, from Lady Apsley, 15 September 1956.

THE GABLES c.1910.

GUY FAWKES PREPARATIONS, 26 October 1963; from left to right, John Colcombe, Alan Hazlewood, Trevor Vick, — ? — Keith Gleed, Graham Vick, Roddy Beasley, Gordon Cook, Andrew Tudor, John Gleed and Andrew Beasley.

A POSTCARD VIEW OF THE STREET c.1900. Note the newly thatched roof. The cottage has since been demolished.

THE VICARAGE c.1901, now a nursing home. The servers and the served, them that served standing on the left, them that were served seated right.

CHILDREN OF CADBURY'S EMPLOYEES at their annual concert c.1925. Back row, left to right; George Abbott, Edith Marsters, Norah Clarke, Vera Daw, Joe Marsters, Frances Taylor, Bob Pamphilon and Harry Marsters. Middle row; Flossie Loomes, Clare Meadows, Jean Westwood, Harry Wilkes, Morag Pamphilon, Winifred Hogg, Monica Halling, Eunice Gibbs, Amy Cottle and Irene Loomes. Elves; Frank Berry, Fred Taylor, Fred Cottle, — ? —, George Tudor. Front row; Beryl Gymer, Joan Tudor, Margaret Westwood, Lily Taylor, — ? —, Enid Abbott, Dorothy Hogg, Mary Berry, Joan Berry and Margot Carter.

FRAMPTON SCHOOLBOYS gardening on part of the allotments which were school gardens, with the headmaster, Tom Osborne, c.1910.

MAY DAY CELEBRATIONS with the children of Cadbury's employees, c.1922. Back row; Lily James, Gladys Longney and Ruth Nicholls. Standing; Steve Attridge, Vera Gymer, Vera Daw, Monica Halling, Morag Pamphilon, Gladys Franklin, Clare Meadows, Frances Taylor and Arthur Stapleton. Kneeling; Gerald Carter, Alan Franklin, Francis Weaver and Arthur Berry. Front row; Leonard Jones, Harry Wilkes, Joan Berry, Edith Marsters (May Queen), Winifred Hogg, Frank Berry and Leslie Weaver.

LIZZIE STOCKHAM, the first lady to bicycle in Frampton; c.1895. Lizzie took over the running of the post office from her father, Nathanial, and retired towards the end of World War II when she was in her seventies.

BUCKHOLT COTTAGES to the right, in this postcard view c.1900.

THE AVENUE IN BETWEEN TREES! Notice the front of Buckholt House; c.1910.

RE-THATCHING FRAMPTON BARN, 26 April 1969.

THE AVENUE, looking back towards the Street, c.1900.

ST. MARY'S, FRAMPTON-ON-SEVERN C.1895. This postcard view shows a small cottage and outbuildings adjacent to the churchyard, with the family taking an interest in the photographer! The cottage was demolished before World War I.

This John Aird & Co. locomotive took gravel from the Frampton-on-Severn pits to barges at Splatt jetty for the Avonmouth Docks when they were being built c.1905. At the jetty the gravel was shot straight from the side tipping hoppers into the barges. George Bowditch, wearing a watch chain, is standing second from left. Charlie Day, white shirted, is close to the rear of the engine.

Tool and storage sheds, used by the men employed at the Frampton gravel pits. Daniel Tudor is standing in the foreground, by the door post on the left hand of the picture, and Charlie Day is sitting, front middle, smoking a cigarette.

FRETHERNE FOOT BEAGLES at Splatt Bridge c.1907, Lionel E. Darell (white breeches) with Jimmy Blakemore to his left.

ON THE SCENT! the FFB beagling through Oatfield and heading towards the village.

Whitminster and Saul

"HOLD IT! WATCH THE BIRDIE AND DON'T MOVE." A photographic record of a Sunday School outing down the Stroudwater Canal towards Saul Junction from Whitminster Wharf c.1900.

AND THEY'RE OFF, at a slow horse pace down the towpath. Wharf House and Wharf Cottage shown on the right hand side. Until recently, both properties remained in the ownership of the Stroudwater Canal Company.

THE WHITMINSTER HOTEL AND THE FORGE c.1900. This picture was on a broken glass negative which we have butted together and printed. Although the negative was damaged, the subject merited reproduction despite the blemishes. The sign above the Forge door begins — A.E. Wyer. The sign in the background, to the left and behind the cycle sign advertises Pratt's Motor Spirit. This sign is now in the bar of the Forge. Albert Wyer obviously catered for motorists from an early date.

THE BERKELEY HUNT meeting at the Whitminster Hotel c.1900. Notice the Georgian style of the building compared to the right-hand picture. The raised parapet has dentil moulding underneath, with a decorated string beneath the first floor windows and a plain string beneath the second floor windows. The style of the façade would suggest a date of 1780-1810 with the building on the left of the picture having been built on slightly later, in a more austere mode. There are also cottages in what is now the hotel car park.

Whitminster Hotel, Glos.

THE WHITMINSTER HOTEL c.1917. A considerable transformation has taken place. The parapet has been removed and the large sash bay windows have been replaced with smaller sashes. The projection covering the front door and first floor window has been completely removed. The whole façade has now been rendered.

Notice the incredible width of the A38 at this time! It still appears to be a dirt road.

THE A38 AT WHITMINSTER 7 April 1971. With the Forge towards the end of its days as a garage, and just before that wonderful £1 note petrol vending machine was installed; a machine that always ignored my new £1 notes and chewed up my old ones! The buildings to the left of the Forge were demolished shortly afterwards.

Left: MR. AND MRS. ALBERT WYER at the Forge. Mr. Wyer was the last blacksmith, and during his time the forge developed as a cycle repair shop and garage. In earlier days the property was a public house named *The Swan*. The motif of a swan is in the top of the timber porch frame.

THE DEMOLITION OF THE OLD POLICE STATION at Whitminster to make way for road widening,
8 February 1967.

CLEANING THE FROME at Whitminster House, 1926.

WHITMINSTER HOUSE with St. Andrew's Church behind, c.1905.

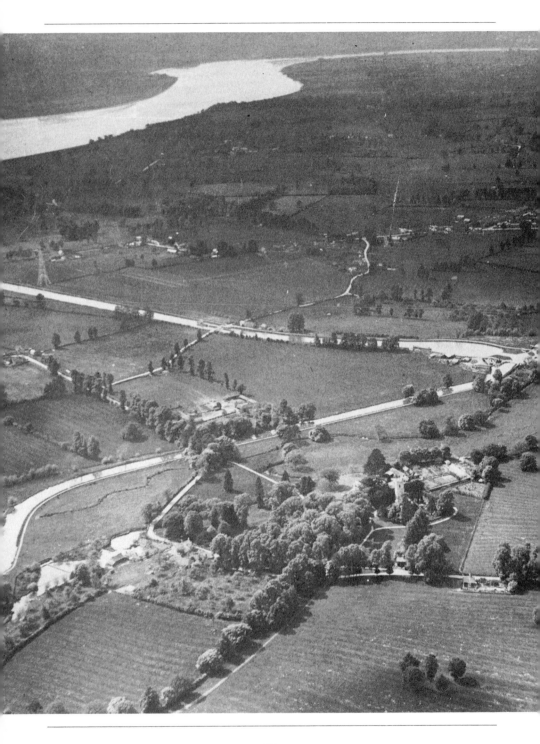

ALL OF THE HORSESHOE, an aerial view of the 1930s or 1940s. An electricity pylon towards the left precludes an earlier date, and the lack of grain store and buildings at Sandfield Bridge precludes it being much later. Can anyone find any visible evidence to give an accurate date? Note the quantity of elm trees before the scourge of Dutch elm disease. Also, the interesting pattern of medieval ridge and furrow. Before the days of enclosure and quickset hedges, the landscape of the Vale was much different. Before the seventeenth and eighteenth centuries much of the land was arable, and not dairy, and the peasants' ridged furlongs are still clearly visible. At the corner of Whitminster Lane, in the bottom right of the picture, it is clear that some form of settlement existed, (shown in the picture with a tree in the middle).

William Marshall writing in 1789 noted that: *'The principal part, or the whole, of the lands of this vale appear to have been, formerly, under the plow; lying, now, in ridge-and-furrow; various as to height and depth. In one instance (at the foot of one of the hills) I observed the ridges, about a rod wide, laid round and high; with a slip, about a yard wide, lying flat between each of them. The ridges were covered with the finest turf, closely pastured; while the intervals were strong beds of rushes. The appearance, at some distance, was singular.'*

The Rural Economy of Glocester-shire.

A MEETING OF THE FRETHERNE FOOT BEAGLES at Whitminster House, 1906. Lionel E. Darell, centre with white breeches, Sir Lionel Darell slightly to his left, also wearing white breeches.

WHITMINSTER WEIR, c.1920.

THE STROUDWATER CANAL at Saul Junction 1953. The Canal was closed to traffic in the following year.

AYLIFFE'S TROW in dry dock at Saul Junction 1890.

A MEETING OF SAUL PARISH COUNCIL in the late 1950s, from left to right; Jack Bourne, Graham Field, Mabel Boucher, Arthur Skuffins, Ken Griffiths, Frank Cookley, Denis Wathen, Reece Silvey and David Thomas.

SAUL JUNCTION c.1910.

ST. JAMES' CHURCH, SAUL with a little girl posing for the photographer, c.1902.

SAUL CHURCH OF ENGLAND SCHOOL, pictured about 1920. The school building shown here was demolished in 1971.

Two views of Saul at the turn of the century, about five years apart, but which comes first? The answer lies in the chimney pots.

A VIEW OF SAUL LOOKING NORTH, c.1902.

Central Stores, Saul.

THE CENTRAL STORES, SAUL c.1920. The shop was closed in 1968 and is now a private house.

THE GREAT FLOODS OF DECEMBER 1965. *Above:* Saul looking north-west. *Right:* Cliff Silvey negotiating the water to get to the garage.

BOATING DOWN THE STREET, Don Lawrence and Felicity Hawkins in the floods of December 1965. The butchers shop behind is now a private house.

Framilode, Epney and Moreton Valence

THE PASSENGER BOAT *LAPWING* making its way down the canal c.1890. This picture was taken from a broken glass negative butted together.

FRAMILODE C.1895, looking north-east towards the Darell Arms and Ayliffe's Mill. The Ayliffe's provided a corn milling service, and at apple time a cider making service using a portable cider press.

THE DARELL ARMS C.1920. One of the few public houses in the area to sell Warn's Beers.

GEORGE LEACH, LICENSEE OF THE DARELL ARMS, 1939-52, ferrying a cyclist over the river to Rodley Sands.

FRAMILODE CHURCH AND VICARAGE c.1900. Both church and vicarage were built by the Darell family in 1854.

CAPTAIN WALTER LONG AND FAMILY c.1900.

TWO PICTURES OF FRAMILODE REGATTA, unfortunately both are damaged. The picture above shows the regatta in one of its last years towards the end of the nineteenth century. The picture below, right, is one of the oldest pictures in the book and dates from 1879, showing the regatta from the other side of the river. The Darell Arms and Ayliffe's Mill on the left are visible, but most other detail is sadly rather indistinct.

NO, NOT CAPTAIN BIRDS EYE, it's Captain Walter Long looking out for pirates from the jetty at the end of his Framilode Tea Garden.

WALTER LONG AND FAMILY outside the tea garden c.1900.

WALTER LONG'S TEA HOUSE – raised on stilts, 1915. Apparently the tea house was susceptible to high tides, and to overcome the problem Walter built a platform eight feet in the air and placed the tea house on top.

SPEEDBOAT RACING ON THE SEVERN at Framilode in 1937. In the top picture the Ayliffe's trow *Irene* can be seen beached up on the bank.

1905 ICE CREAM VENDOR at the south-west side of Walter Long's Riverside Tea Gardens.

THE VICTORIA TEMPERANCE HOTEL AND TEA GARDENS at the Pridings, Framilode c.1901.

These two photographs come from the same negative, taken in 1901. I could not resist putting both to demonstrate the postcard vendor's licence. The top picture is natural with the sails of the boats disappearing in the background. The bottom, rather surreal picture has been heavily touched up and re-photographed.

This picture, although rather poor in quality shows the site of the Framilode Passage Ferry with Walter Long's jetty in the background.

SALMON FISHING in the Severn at Framilode, c.1895.

Above and below, left and right: Four views of the junction of the Stroudwater Canal with the River Severn. Now completely filled in, it is only with difficulty that you can trace the area shown in these evocative photographs.

Framilode, The Canal Bridge (open)

Below: Tom Ayliffe's boat *Irene,* he used this boat to ferry grain from Avonmouth to Framilode for the mill.

Above: A narrow boat on the Stroudwater Canal at Moor Street.

*Right: ROSE c.*1935. This boat was used to ferry tar from Stroud Gas Works and was one of the last boats to use the stretch of the Stroudwater Canal between Saul Junction and Framilode.

THE ANCHOR AT EPNEY c.1930 showing the 'Stroud Brewery Ales' sign. Notice the road at this time, an area constantly flooded at high tide.

A CLOSE-UP OF THE ANCHOR c.1945 showing the south side having been rendered, and the sign 'zipped-up' to an ultra-modern bold sans-serif style to advertise 'Stroud Ales'.

DAVID THOMAS AND NIGEL LONGNEY outside the Anchor. Nigel was junior fishing champion with this prize eel, 5 October 1968.

THE MORETON VALENCE CAFE, closed and demolished in the 1970s to make way for three new houses. Photograph c.1940.

TWO HOUSES AT MORETON VALENCE (since demolished) c.1925. Notice the width and surface of the A38 at this time.

Above: CASTLE BRIDGE, EPNEY c.1925. The trow is the *Epney Lass* owned by the Silveys of Epney, and built about 1869.
Below: MR. W.H. BUTT AND HIS DAUGHTER MOLLY in a dog trap outside Marshfield Farm, Epney, c.1925.

THE CITY OF GLOUCESTER FIRE FLOAT *SALAMANDER* on its inauguration day, 12 July 1906. The following year the Salamander proved itself in fighting arson attacks at Nicks, Griggs and Price Walker's timber yards.

HAYWAINS AND RICK at Riverside Farm, Epney c.1920. James Butt moved here from Court Farm, Arlingham. Notice the painted lettering on the second wagon.

Longney, Elmore and Hardwicke

LONGNEY AFC, 1925. Back row, left to right; Les Leach, Sam Harris, 'Podding' Leach, Arthur Clarke, Charlie Butt and Stan Bullock. Front row; Teddy Ellis, Arthur Smith, Jimmy Webb 'Shinell' Bayliss and Teddy Browning.

THE HORSEPOOLS AND LONGNEY CHURCH, 11 February 1974.

THE INTERIOR OF ST. LAURENCE'S CHURCH, LONGNEY, 1902. This medieval church was restored by F.S. Waller in 1873.

ELVER FISHING AT ELMORE BACK, April 1901.

BOW LANE FARMHOUSE, LONGNEY c.1895. This farmhouse was the home of the Palmer family from the early seventeenth century until 1890. It was demolished in the 1930s.

FLOODS AT ELMORE BACK, February 1926.

THREE GENERATIONS OF THE WEBB FAMILY of Minsterworth when the old Roman street, now Church Lane was flooded c.1909. This picture is cheating a little as it is just over the river, but the scene is quite evocative. From the left in the boat, Ted Webb (with paddle), with his sons, William (centre boat), and Frederick. Watching them from the garden of Snowdrop Cottage, is Beatrice, Frederick's wife, and their son Ted.

THE SEVERN BORE, a photograph taken in 1901 looking across to Stonebench from the Minsterworth side.

HARDWICKE BRIDGE c.1925. Note the house on the right; built to the same blueprint as Kimberley House, Frampton, near Fretherne Bridge.

THE S.S. *RIVER AVOCA* of Cardiff nearing Hardwicke *c.*1920.

ST. NICHOLAS CHURCH, HARDWICKE 1905.

A MEETING OF THE BERKELEY HUNT AT HARDWICKE COURT, 21 November 1959. Miss Olive Lloyd Baker at the back.

The construction of the Cross Keys Roundabout at Hardwicke to tie in with the building of the M5 and the north-bound Gloucester south exit, 15 August 1970.

Quedgeley
and
Hempsted

ONE OF THE EARLIER PHASES OF CONSTRUCTION AT QUEDGELEY, Fieldcourt Estate, 26 November 1974.

ST. JAMES' CHURCH, QUEDGELEY C.1904. The tower and spire are 14th century, but the church itself was largely rebuilt in 1856 by H. Woodyer.

LOOKING SOUTH DOWN THE A38 AT QUEDGELEY C.1930.

Two views of the demolition of the munitions factory at Quedgeley in 1926. The factory was built during World War I.

THE AVENUE, QUEDGELEY c.1910. A scene that has undergone one or two slight changes in recent years.

Not much was left of this lorry after an accident on the A38 at Quedgeley in 1926.

WITNESS THE FIELDS! An aerial view of Hardwicke and Quedgeley, 1961.

PEGGING OUT THE ROUTE! Phase one of the construction of the new Bristol Road roundabout, 20 February 1968.

A COTTAGE AT REA LANE HEMPSTED, c.1905.

THE CROSS, HEMPSTED c.1880.

A WEEKLY RATTING EXPEDITION at the corporation rubbish tip at Hempsted, 1926.

AN AERIAL VIEW OF HEMPSTED,
looking north, 1961.

THE POST OFFICE AT HEMPSTED c.1904.

ST. ANNE'S WELL, HEMPSTED, 1901.